IT'S ONLY PAPER
An Unlikely Anthology

"Poets are the midwives of reality"

– John Keats

IT'S ONLY PAPER

An Unlikely Anthology

Derek L. Dugan
R.M. Kent
Vincent D. Pisano
Gabor J. Szabo

Yggdrasil Press
New Milford, CT
2009

Copyright © 2009 by Vincent D. Pisano
All Rights Reserved
Manufactured in the United States of America

Published by Yggdrasil Press
www.yggdrasilpress.com
www.myspace.com/yggdrasilpress

Poets Anonymous
www.myspace.com/anonymouspress

Library of Congress Catalog Card Number: Pending
ISBN 978-0-578-02915-3

First Printing: May 2009

Edited by Vincent D. Pisano

Cover Photograph by Gabor J. Szabo
Cover Design by Vincent D. Pisano

Contents

"The Ghetto in the Meadow"   9

Poems

Block	15
Oubliette	16
The Minstrel and the Lyre	17
Veni, Vedi, Arriverderci	18
Rain	19
A Fresh-Red Kill	21
Riky Tiky Tik	23
Ashes	25
Her Waves	27
Roxanne of My Own	28
Taken	29
Flakes of Ash	30
My Delilah	32
Loathéd	34
Nepenthe	36
Yourself to Save	37
The Ballad of Mr. Hyde	39
Ant Hill	42
Crescent City Son	44
No Mor	45
Janus-side	46
Breach	48
Twilight	50

Sum?	51
Sapphic Eden	53
This is What I Think of Your Exercise	54
Let Go	55
In Case You Didn't Know	56
[The Color of] Louisiana Steam	57
Hip-Hop: To My Mother	58
No Partise Anum	62
Mason Dixon, Sr.	64
Illusions	65
Fading	67
Listless Years	69
It's Only Paper	70
Reflections	72
Transcendence	73
Avise la Fin?	75
Cracked Rearview	77
Dryad's Dirge	78
Passion	79
Acknowledgements	81
About the Authors	83
Index of Poetry by Authors	85

"The Ghetto in the Meadow"

We needed our fix. Like clockwork our cars climbed the steep, dirt slope to the small New Preston cabin, not far from Lake Waramaug. Sometimes the scenery changed: a warehouse in Danbury, a smoking-den basement in New Milford, an aged apartment in Gaylordsville with exposed hand-hewn beams. But usually our cars rocked back and forth on the protruding stones and the rain gouged trenches of this inconspicuous driveway, our axles violently bottoming out as we ascended to the plateau before the homely cabin. Its foundation an old swimming pool, the structure seemed a mishmash of mismatched buildings combined into a single small abode, surrounded by overgrown weeds that grazed our knees as we approached.

Its interior smelled of the smoke that wafted from the mouths, nostrils and ashtray offerings scattered about. Gabor was assigned the task of mixing the elixir they craved, that they would consume until their hands shook with nervous jitters. Martin laid out the latest stash for our hungry eyes to feed upon, and we in turn placed our contributions onto the small table which we gathered around. For the past week our addiction continually resurfaced in the forefront of our minds, a gnawing beast that occupied our daily tasks and dug detouring burrows into the paths of our every thought.

Gabor returned with the coffee, handing a cup to Derek. Martin took a drag from his cigarette and flicked it over the ashtray. I remained content with a cold soda and began reading my latest piece. It was a Sunday evening like those previous of the past two years. It was Poets Anonymous. Like the alcoholics program from which our title was inspired, we each shared the accomplishments and setbacks of the previous week. In turn, it was the listeners' duty to lend their support and critical analysis, offering assistance and suggestions when possible.

Since the summer of 2004 the small group has attracted fellow verse-addicts and listeners. Armed only with caffeine, we would read, consider, and laugh into the early morning hours, leaving us with a sense of satisfaction, but an insatiable craving throughout the week ahead. Two other such peers, Meghan and Amanda, who were with us through the early months of Poets Anonymous, also have each a poem featured in this work.

The magic of language and the allure of words fascinate and invigorate us all. In solitary such power can be deafening and unwieldy, leading one to impossible writers' blocks or bloated pieces in need of shedding their excess weight. However, when shared it can be harnessed and reined, subdued and shaped into the rare thing of beauty it is: poetry.

Soon, Sundays were not enough. Throughout the summer of 2005 we sponsored a Poetry Open Mic Night in Marbledale, CT, where we could read our pieces to a larger audience and appreciate the works of others. And the numbers quickly swelled, attracting like-minded individuals who were nevertheless as unique as the art-form they loved. However, when one has a problem with addiction, they can never be satisfied long.

Hence we decided to create this book. It will hopefully offer a flavor, if not the very excitement we feel in not only creating these poems, but also in exposing them to new readers who may understand or directly relate to the pieces. We desire to contribute something special on a personal level to the reader, as well as an artistic one to the local community. Poetry is special, beautiful, and most importantly – relevant. It speaks to us, to the very core of our being by offering vignettes into our lives, windows into our minds, and doorways into our own human condition.

Vincent D. Pisano
New Milford, CT
January, 2009

Poems

Block
R.M. Kent

Wrought in a wicked weave of verse,
Far worse than the thickest
Thistledown.

Caught in the working mind immersed,
In thirst for the Quickest
Query 'round;
I pounce on words like money found.

Wrapped in a sickness, seized in tense
And fenced in a frigid
Fruitless-ground.

Trapped in a torrid tease immense,
Intent on the richest
Riddled sound;

Oubliette
Vincent D. Pisano

The walls of blocks are hours thick
    From time I've spent to idly sit
And stare at a page still lifeless and bare,
    Until tired eyes burn, and I no longer care.

And its rickety roof of loosely laid wood
    Where upon clear nights alone I stood
And viewed my world from a distance afar.
    Finding no place, I reached to the stars.

White plain with blue veins, and my black line to sever
    And loop into letters
And shed the scabs of a passionate leper,
    The blood of this heart-broke confessor.

Seeking a reason to find
    A riddle calling, another rhyme,
All to catch a glimpse of a beauty so rare,
    Until tired hearts yearn, and I no longer care.

The Minstrel and the Lyre
Derek L. Dugan

In fields of dew with grass of green
   Morning breaks upon the stone,
When to its edge a man does stride
   Who thinks his thoughts alone.

For solitude is what he wants,
   Or at least that's what he'll state,
But works he's done he still does deal
   And to them we relate.

And all this time he'll spend the day
   Till shadows cast the setting sun.
He'll pour his heart into his piece
   Of which he gladly shuns.

And what he knows we cannot say,
   But songs of his may yet inspire.
His words are notes with parchment strings,
   This minstrel plays the liar.

Veni, Vedi, Arrivederci
R.M. Kent

I went to the woods,
   With the clothes on my back,
With pen and paper and canvas sac;
   I went to the woods – to write.

I stayed in the woods,
   With the fire I built,
With pen and paper and camping quilt;
   I stayed in the woods – at night.

I dwelt in the woods,
   With the words in my head,
With pad of paper and pen gone dead;
   I dwelt in the woods – all night.

I came from the woods,
   With the clothes on my back,
With camping quilt and canvas sac;
   I came from the woods – to write.

Rain
Gabor J. Szabo

      Smoking thoughts and burnt effigies
      Spiraling
      High into the sky.

Dream of thunder,
Of Rain
Falling,
Cascading.
Emotions swelling every drop,
Exploding on naked shoulders.

      Smoking thoughts and burnt effigies

Dancing 'round a pyre,
Wooden column burning,
Offered to the gods.
War paint, tribal drums
Pleading, chanting.
Beat quickening,
Flames roaring,

      Spiraling.

In the belly of night,
What you can see
And cannot,
Silhouettes and creatures
Lurking, hunting, waiting,
Hiding.

Night morphing,
It is why I dance,
Why my pyre burns,
For fortune

    High into the sky.

A Fresh-Red Kill
Vincent D. Pisano

With weapons I trekked down mountainside
    To go hunt in the wild dell,
And stealthily search the forestry
    Tracking a scent I smelled.

My impatience grew with passing time,
    I wandered the wood for days;
My path was made by several trails for
    Each turn led me astray.

In clearing I saw the beast I sought,
    Notched my arrow on the bow,
And putting my eyes beside the fletch
    Pointed it where to go.

With quick *twang* the thirsty missile flew
    And then pierced its hairy side,
Sending the animal fleeing fast
    Searching a place to hide.

I followed its blood for many suns,
    Found it lay with slowing breath
And shot my flint-tip into its heart,
    Ending what fight was left.

But my work was only half complete
    For I had to bring it home
So I hacked the limbs with my stone axe
    And stripped wet flesh from bone.

Up the mountain I returned again
      With a tale to tell half-true,
And to share with all a fresh-read kill –
      This poem I've read to you.

Riky Tiky Tik
R.M. Kent

Riky, tiky, tiky
Riky, tiky, tik
An ol' chevy van
Goin' riky tiky tik

Racin' on the hi-way
Traffic kinda' thik
My ol' steady hand
Goin' riky tiky tik

Rushin' to my lover
Gotta get there quik
My romantic heart
Goin' riky tiky tik

I know she's a-waitin'
Toe-ing tappy tip
Bless her little head
Goin' riky tiky tik

Bring a dozen roses
Always does the trik
Gets her little hooch
Goin' riky tiky tik

Later in the evenin'
Playin tat for tit
A four-poster bed
Goin' riky tiky tik

After she's a-sleepin'
Burnin up the wik
An ol' type-writer's
Goin' riky tiky tik

Riky, tiky, tiky
Riky, tiky, tik
My poetic soul
Goin' riky, tiky, tik

Ashes
Derek L. Dugan

I hold a candle
   In the cold dark night.
Will I mishandle
   This keeper of light?

I wanna wield it
   And its burning flame.
Desires submit,
   This world I will maim.

      Kick up the ashes, see inside of me.

I stand for vengeance
   And I stand for pain.
I am defiance
   That you can't contain.

Terrible bastard
   Without a soul.
And empty hazard,
   Of dark burning coal.

      Kick up the ashes, see inside of me.

Now you see in me
   How the embers glow.
Fear to follow me
   On this path I've chose.

King of misery
   Wears a worthless crown.
Flames inside of me
   Torch this world to the ground.

Her Waves
Gabor J. Szabo

Black glazen boulders and
  Pebbles turned by tide,
Waves crashing alcoves and
  Caves carved by time.

Blue silky surface and
  Satin lace on sea,
Winds calling surges of
  Urges deep in glee.

Black shrouded shoulders and
  Flashes of her eyes,
Waves dancing golden hair
  Gathered 'round her guise.

Blue silky covers and
  Satin lace on thighs,
Sin surfing fingers
      Plying what's inside.

Roxanne of My Own
Vincent D. Pisano

A secret admirer, the romantic that I am,
I never thought that I should have my very own Roxanne.
My nose if not a beak, so the deformities I shield
Are letters I have written that I never can reveal.

My wit though be it sound, perhaps there's beauty I still lack,
Tis still that I become the modern day De Bergerac.
And so my world becomes Frankland, and my long coat a cape,
This pen my sword to parry for the pride I keep at stake.

Yet maybe I should tell her, though a Christian I am not,
The passion fires that burn and swell; such things my Hell hath wrought.
Because when my chapter's over, and the Fates turn the page,
Will it come to be that both our ends too will be the same?

So I'll untie my treacherous tongue and speak with grace and zeal,
Before this character I've become is all I truly am
And the plot that locks our lives fatally grows too real.

Taken
R.M. Kent

Oh lover won't you take me
    Where you took me once before
  Under milky moonlight
     Where the sea becomes the shore

I never can remember
    Having ever loved you more
Oh lover won't you take me
    In the sea-oats by the shore

Oh lover let me take you
    Where I took you once before
  Beyond palatial pines
    Where the water comes ashore

Forever I'll remember
    Having never loved you more
Oh lover let me take you
    On the sea-oats by the shore

Flakes of Ash
Gabor J. Szabo

Not a breeze to stir
Among the trees,
Gentle plume of smoke, rising.
Bits of ash lighter than snowflakes,
Results of what once was.

Leaves blurry in commotion,
Confusing the confusion with sense.
Memories and emotions cascading,
              The source ignites –

    My fingers number one thousand,
    All I touch becomes fuel
    And as I digest the forest
    The breath I give is a cloud of soot.

    My chaotic senses whisper,
    She is almost within reach,
    I hunger to caress her
    With my gentle, choking smoke.

Look in the eyes,
Study the reflections,
Her eyebrows and lips.
I can sing to her
Of many things, bitter and sweet,
Of my image in her eye
Or the cauldron in me
Glowing with the longing for

All that she tries to hide.

Her placid surface
Hiding rituals of decay below.
Her breath feeds my inferno
Yet I cannot eat away her rotting insides…

Among the burnt out trunks
A gentle plume of smoke, billowing
Flakes of ash:
Foretellers of what is to come,
The breeze begins to stir.

My Delilah
Derek L. Dugan

Hello,
Can you hear me!
And will you listen to me?
   As I tell a tale
   Of the time we spent,
Wondering what might have been.

There,
Can you see me!
And will you look right through me?
   To the other side,
   Of the consequence,
Worrying what might have been.

Now,
Can you feel me!
And know what you've done to me?
   You betrayed my trust
   With no moral sense,
Not caring what might have been.

       Say now did you hear me laughing,
       And tell me did you see me cry?
       I know that you have seen me smiling,
       But have you ever had to hear me lie?
       Did you really have to hear me asking
       To know you've never seen me hide?
       I wonder did you see me trying,

    So tell me did you feel me die?

What,
About reason;
And what about all your lies?
  What about feeling…

  All these what abouts
And all they might have been.

Loathéd
Vincent D. Pisano

I thought you were mistaken
    When you crept into my bed,

        But you laid yourself beside me,
            Fluffed a pillow for your head,
            And you did not turn the lamp on
        To leave the room dark instead.

I thought you'd be disgusted
    When you felt me beneath the sheets,

        But you pressed your breasts against my chest
            To feel how fast hearts beat
            And smeared your sap across my knee
        As you crawled to lower heat.

I thought you would be repulsed
    When you found that the warmth was mine,

        But your hands felt with intention
            The length of my hairy thighs
            And gripped my pulse in a loving fist
        To coax what's kept inside.

I thought you would be regretful
    When morning exposed my face,

        But you gave a gift of gentle kiss
            And looked with wond'rous gaze,

And I watched you walk to the bathroom door…

Just like yesterday.

Nepenthe
Gabor J. Szabo

What troubles brew in nights unslept?
Love hangs in the gallows, no tears must be wept.

Truth be reckoned, our Troy burnt to ground
By manifold fears our doubting youth found.

Flew too high and sentenced to hell,
I am scattered on grounds where Icarus fell.

Deeply asunder, losing redemption,
A wounded love dies from human deception.

Now my cause is tethered before
Harlot's foul dealings in a single night's lore.

My truth is made of a suffering zeal:
I find this to be mankind's Achilles heel.

Yourself to Save
Derek L. Dugan

You sit alone at the kitchen table
   And wish it were a dream.
Your eyes are bruised and his mind's unstable,
   It's not as bad as it seems.

      If you had to make a choice today,
      Would you run or would you stay?

When times are tough and the money's tight,
   It always seems it's your fault.
The liquor flows and his temper will rise,
   He then begins his assault.

      Live in fear until your dying day –
      The rain is cold, the sky is gray.

How many times have you heard that bullshit,
   Trying to make his amends?
Says he's sorry and he didn't mean it,
   "It won't happen again."

      The trust you gave that was betrayed,
      Will you go on living this charade?

Your crying out for those things you have lost:
   Pride, trust, the child within.
Without a choice you always pay the cost,
   Know now what you should have then –

Being beaten just like a slave,
Nothing's left except yourself... to save.

The Ballad of Mr. Hyde
R.M. Kent

Well he wanted to be Jekyll
But his name was Mr. Hyde
There was something he was tryin to say
All locked up deep inside
Though he longed to let it out
When he tried his – tongue got tied
So he drank and he sank
And while drunk he – thunk
And almost got out what it was about
But he couldn't – maybe he shouldn't
And the more he sought
The more distraught he became
Could it be he – simply
Was the same

So he smoked and he choked
And he did not find
The seed of need that was in his mind
And after the toke he tried the coke
It shook his coat but did not take
The beast away – there was still
Something he was tryin to say
One day came a man
Who knew the plan – or so he said
Try this, can't miss – untwist your head
He tripped and fell – saw a glimpse of hell
He laughed and cried – He'd seen inside

So he climbed to the chimes to the top

Of the tallest steeple in the town
And began to shout what it was all about
To the people on the ground
"Gather round – hear my sound
My truth is profound – I'll be renowned"
Then looking down he found to his astound
No one looking up from the ground
"Don't they care – can't they see
My soul is bare – I've been set free"
As he shed a tear – his worse fear
Became clear – they simply could not hear
He could finally say – what needed saying
Could finally be – what being needed
But he was missin someone to listen
None to hear his desperate diction
There he cried – brains all fried
And decided to climb back inside
But just as he tried – he started to slide –
And as fate would have it his grasp was denied
And down on the ground
They finally heard his sound
It was too late – he was earth bound
But just before he crashed he cried –
"I AM…" Then slam – he smashed and died
They rushed around and found him there –
But all they did was stand and stare
Fore there upon the earth and stone
Lie his lifeless flesh and bones
But what they couldn't sense or see
Was that he – was finally free

And so my friends – my story ends

The gravitation of the situation
Couldn't be denied
But at least we heard, his beastly words
And so goes the ballad
Of – Mr. Hyde

Ant Hill
Gabor J. Szabo

Vast oceans churning,
Creatures, primitive yearning.
I was wondering
What planet I was seeing.

Spread throughout the land,
On two legs they stand,
Cities made by their hands,
Linked by luminous strands.

Called "humans", I am hearing,
Race young and fleeting,
Brains still growing,
Uncertain future I was thinking.

Passionate and emotional,
Crude yet functional,
Hateful to none but all-
Arrogant yet… so small.

This I find interesting:
So bent on loving,
And on destroying,
But somehow still living.

Full of literature,
On paper they measure,
Their societies pleasure,
And sins of rapture.

But, I am ending
My study: "The human being,"
So small and pleasing –
> **They will make an easy killing**

Crescent City Son
Vincent D. Pisano

What happen to th' music?
Where's it gone?
Days gone by
Since I seen ma lawn.
   Ain't played me no jazz,
   Ain't heard me no song.
   I heah only black water,
   An th' sound is all wrong.

What happen to ma baby?
Where she gone?
Days gone by,
It seem like so long.
   Dint want ta let go,
   I tried to be strong,
   But I'm heah alone,
   An black waters flow on.

What happen to th' angels?
Where they gone?
Days gone by,
No one come along.
   Ain't got me no home,
   No where I belong,
   Black water it soaks me,
   An I can't hold on.

No Mor
R.M. Kent

I don't wanna pay
  for yor bullets no mor
I don't wanna pay it no mor

I don't wanna fund
  yor political war
I don't wanna fund it no mor

      In five hundred years
        they been five hundred wars
      th' next five hundred
        'll see five hundred mor

I don't wanna grease
  yor war machine
I don't wanna grease it no mor

I don't wanna see
  no dyin no mor
I don't wanna see it no mor

      I seen widowed wives
        an seen orphaned mothers
      seen fathers an sons
        a-killin' they brothers

An I don't wanna see
  no mor – no mor
I don't wanna see it no mor!

Janus-Side
Gabor J. Szabo

Give me your vindictive discrimination,
Give me the flesh of oppressed,
Give me your biblical annihilation,
Give me your hatred transgressed.

Entertain the troubadour of death,
Entertain the cyclical plague,
Entertain the evil in your breath,
Entertain the morality vague.

Now I will kill a whole generation,
Now I will turn your eyes bleak,
Now I am the bane of creation,
Now I delight hunting meek.

Open your hatred and prosper,
Open your mind's twisted will,
Open your hunger for slaughter,
Open your instinct to kill.

Care not for humanity lacking,
Care not for mass starvation,
Care not for willful attacking,
Care not for planned elimination.

I created your indecisions,
I created your killing arts,
I created your missing provisions,
I created the fear in your hearts.

Death in the eyes of the ordained,
Death in the inhuman masquerade,
Death in the fate of those named,
Death in the psychotic charade.

Enter the flames of the Inquisition,
Enter the showers filling with gas,
Enter the Nyarubuye Mission,
Enter the butchering of the mass.

Breach
Meghann O'Donnell

charlatan! fraudulent and pomp!
stomping over Sacred Ground and
Waterways and Dignity!
careening and canteening upon
Love and Life and Meaning
and on Pride! The Force Inside!
intimidators! domineers!
Relinquish yr constraint and Liberate!
do not negate the Cry that Rises
for We have the Drive Inside Us
We can Strive and We Can Thrive
and We Can Get Up when We fall! No Chance too small!
malaise is normalcy these Days and
passing on the haze We're losing
any Sight of Hope or Height or
Light to Guide Us Thru the Night!
Our Way is lost!
We can't afford the cost!
blackmailed, blackballed,
thru ignorance We pay it all
We claim it all, We Say it all,
and Passion-less We slay it all
can any part We Save at all?
no Reckoning is made! no Role unplayed!
But wait…
You cannot tell Me it's too late
don't inundate with hopeless Fate
for We Can Break This Weight and Rise
and We Can Open Up Our Eyes

and We Can Reach
   You kno, if We Can Reach, then We Can Breach…

Twilight
Derek L. Dugan

Pain divided,
   The heart skips a beat.
Darkness engulfing,
   Sorrow in defeat.

The long halls traveled –
   No end, no ray of light.
Blood spilling steel:
   The never-ending fight.

Death in creation,
   Life in decay,
Comfort in delusions –
   Push it all away.

Confusion in a wish,
   Pull stars from the sky.
Heart pumping hurt,
   Just say goodbye.

Sum?
Gabor J. Szabo

I
The me,
The you in me.
I say,
I think therefore,
I am.

I like that,
I see that,
I think that.
I

It's good to be confident in yourself,
So they say to me.
Of course,
It's not hard to be confident in me,
Just one person.
I

I am not selfish.
Funny, huh?
I am not selfish because that's bad to others,
Soo… it is good to be unselfish
Because it does not hurt others.
Therefore I will be good selfish
So I will be un-selfish so **I** do not hurt others.
I

So many problems from the "I."

We think so much of ourselves.
I have this problem, and this one, and that one, and…
The "I" forms into your universe.
You wonder why it all falls apart so easily.
World won't tick to everyone's own clock,
The clock of "I."

Be confident in others.
Be selfish to others.
Think of someone else's problems.
What you have going on is nothing.
You are just one of 6.8 billion "I"s.
Can we even comprehend that number?

We can't separate our "I" from us,
But maybe we can make a difference in others.
Not just in our own, self created, mad universe,
And notice that the key to us
Is I.

Sapphic Eden
Vincent D. Pisano

Dew upon the tu lips,
   Petals moist and wet,
Dripping from the tender tips
   The place where life begets.

She loves to feel such pretty things,
   Deeply she inhales their scent.
Warm and exposed, she spreads them wide
   To make way for taste descent.

Nectar salt and honey sweet,
   She swallows all she can squeeze,
And lies down again between slender stems;
   Soundly in the garden she sleeps.

This Is What I Think Of Your Exercise
Derek L. Dugan

Write Haiku for you?
Known to you, this is untrue –
No Haiku, fuck you!

Let Go
R.M. Kent

Ever since I can remember
I saved things beyond their use
And I kept them in my closet
On the shelves or lying loose

Packed all up in little boxes
Tossed in jars and on the floor
So much stuff I stored together
Til I couldn't close the door

Ever since I can remember
I saved things I should let go
Til I break and clean my closet
And a weight lifts from my soul

Even now although I'm older
All that baggage takes its toll
Well today I cleaned my closet
And I thought I'd let you know

In Case You Didn't Know
Derek L. Dugan

I thought I could love,
   But I gave into hate.

I tried to understand,
   But I could not relate.

I thought I was strong,
   But I learned I could feel.

I tried to fight back,
   But nothing seemed real.

I thought I forgave,
   But who's wrong or right?

I tried to believe,
   But I just said good night.

[The Color of] Louisiana Steam
Vincent D. Pisano

"Bad girl, bad girl," she told herself,
And beat her brow with tiny fists.
They could tell her that it was someone else,
But her little conscience would persist.

Blood puddles in the wheat, she never liked its sight.
Red roses bloom on her floral dress,
They are the color of the state of her mind.
But daisies were her favorite, the little one must confess.

Louisiana steam, melting pot at boil,
Words were spoken, teeth are scattered.
Lilies always seemed so pure (the millipede recoils).
She never liked black roses,
        They never really mattered.

Hip-Hop: To My Mother
Amanda Armstrong

My mother listens to hip-hop.
Guns pop rhymes drop
Consant chronic crops on a Harlem rooftop
And it won't stop until the final bullet drops
In the chest
Of the last emcee.
Heads of rows and fros bob while cristal flows
Dutch smoke blows
Black men behavin like Dumbo's crows.
More ho's
Crawl out of my mother's cd player
Than stand on every street in Los Angeles.
And the money grows.

While ethnicity's erased defaced
Replaced by the impurity of the majority
Promisin celebrity prosperity publicity
For the minority of the minority
Who in egocentricity
Can't see they have no dignity
The forced invisibility of their own nationality
The cause of the contumely of our hopeful posterity
Won't see that the integrity
Of an entire generation
Of African-Americans
Has been snuffed out
By the sole of corporate America.
I hear hip-hop take its dying breath
Through the crackle

Of my mother's speakers.

Mom,
I say,
You know there's better hip-hop?
With political thought analytical phrase
Made by radicals who are
Socially-conscious?
Hip-hop that is out to change the world?

Your hip-hop has no beat,
She says,
Your music has no soul.
I am the social-conscious.
You were not there.
You did not wait at Woolworth's while every white was waited on before you.
You were not dragged to the back of the bus
Not knowing Georgia was not Jersey and you were a second rate second grader second class citizen
In a first world country with third world conditions.
You were not there.

You were not there the day Emmet Till was dragged from his bed
Not knowing that south side Chicago was not south side America
Where the justice of the third world reigned.

You were never trained to be contained
To be restrained
By the ingrained limitations

Of your race
That your place was preordained.

You did not march with Martin/Malcolm/Marcus
You did not sing with Marvin/Mayfield/Marley
And you did not cry the day they died.
You did not see your pride denied.
You were not told you must abide
You did not have to hide
What could not be expressed
Without fear of arrest or death for your protest
Of a system you detest.

You were not there.

You have never seen a black panther.
You have never seen a klansmember.

You say you remember Amadou
While shitting in a diaper
And I'm spitting at the t.v.
19 bullets ripped through his chest
Cops slay the oppressed they detest
At the request of the majority
Another black man laid to rest.

At best
You were chewing on your toes
While the LAPD remained restrained as blacks and Koreans entertained the mass
Killing each other in the streets of Los Angeles
Maintaining containing

Eliminating
The bad element.

You did not wake when the media faked
Concern for James Byrd
Dragging chained to a truck
Making race yet again a four-letter word.
The South is to blame
The media claimed
Not the same in the North we are tame
It's a shame
Another black man's pain
Another one slain
And yet I still sustain.

So you can have your socially-conscious hip-hop.
But I am socially-conscious hip-hop's mother superior.
And I like my music with a beat.
With a soul.

No Partise Anum
R.M. Kent

Hand-shakey firmly
    Kissy poo poo
Takey booty, hidey-hole

So feely mondo
    Importanto
Like a honcho, yet not so-so

Likey horsies
    Wagon harness
Breakey spirit – thinky honest

All inversus
    And perverseness
Thinky maybe, even worseness

Rising lately
    Sleeping wakey
Drinky coffee – even cold

Makey wonder
    Where asunder
Dreamy youth did ever go

Under looky
    Catchy gist
Thinky surface – this you miss

Deep in sleepy

Where we weepy
Unbeknownst to even us

Creatures creepy
   Underneathy
Biding time – 'til risey up

With-each within
   There hidey cowards
Monsters, villuns, heroes too

Ever waiting
   Even baiting
Turn us grown-ups, me an' you

So keepy vigil
   All your days
And you hidey beings at bay

Or wakey one day
   Wond'rin why
The adults out –
   An' you're inside

Mason Dixon, Sr.
Gabor J. Szabo

Troubles o' th' mynd,
D'cisions o' th' day,
Bin bogged down o' late.

Perplex'd n' confus'd,
Th' ans'es nevah seem cleah,
Enahgy beset bah waste,
Tho' ah see it cleah
Don't mean ah c'n change it.

When ahm on th' road,
In mah bed,
Setin' in th' rockah,
D'cisions lay heavy
Lahk a Judg's wood'n mallet.
Why d'cide n' act when
Nothin' seems too cleah?

Waitin' fo' th' sto'ms t' fade,
Last drop o' rain t' scape
Last day o' gray.
Waitn's a d'cision…

But why wait fo' a d'cision
Whin d'cision's all ah c'n make,
Whin any d'cision's a' stake?

Illusions
Derek L. Dugan

I still recall the days that fade away…
    Searching for the words, yet
        Not knowing what to say
My dreams and memories, they cloud my sight…
    Walking down a path, that
        Disappears in the night
Hopes and aspirations of long before…
    Gone and forgotten, still
        They worry ever more

    Everywhere I go
        They're all I see
            Everyone I am
                They're all I'll be

During all of this time I've wondered how…
    Lost where I've wandered, and
        Just where I've come to now
Rapt within my mind with no sound or shape…
    Endless void of night, I'm
        Accepting no escape
These pages of the book for all to see…
    One more painful way, that
        They're forced to remind me

                Every time I hurt
            They're all I feel
        Nothing as it seems
    Illusions all to real

Telling the diff'rence is so hard to say…
        Even though I tried, still
                It all just fades away
Reality lost only pain remains…
        Holding on no more, thus
                My sanity's been slain
Falling further down while no hands will lend…
        Lost and forsaken, now
                I've reached my spiral's end

Fading
Vincent D. Pisano

In the deep oaken drawer of an attic chest
   I found a lost picture of long neglect.

What was once monotone, now yellowed with age,
   I wiped the dust from this faded page.

And in this old photograph there were posed three –
   The portrait of a family.

      First there stood a towering man, crowned top hat black
      With a bow-tie tuxedo and coat tails to match.
      His gaze was straight forward, while his hair was slicked back
      And his moustache hooked upward with the help of bee's wax.

      At about waist high was a child girl
      With energetic eyes and russet copper curls,
      Upon which was set a dainty bonnet
      With numerous little flowers placed decoratively on it.

      And to the side was a woman: a mother and wife
      Of Romanesque beauty still prime in her life.
      Sitting solemnly stiff in umbrellic shade
      Attired with baby's breath, and soft ribbons of lace.

I returned the moment, that brief glimpse of time,
   Into its home where the light never shines.

Enclosed in its cask and enveloped by dark,
  Forgotten again as memories are.

Another reminder what to all shall be –
  Fading into obscurity.

Listless Years
Gabor J. Szabo

The hollow shell of another year
Cracks and caves in with a thunder.
Thrashing like a newborn stream at winters end,
Feelings stabbing like a frost-ridden wind.

Spring rolls in as thunder from the distance,
Daftly punching holes in what was paper protecting a soul frail,
Slowly reverberating like passing storms always do.
I am scattered like marbles dropped on cobblestone sidewalk.

A black hole comes forth with the creeping Summer shadow,
Sucking and devouring at everything with intensity.
I shuffle and limp, a prisoner with his ball and chain,
The clasp ripping into the ankle, into the flesh, scraping the bone.

Clouds are cast as Autumn crawls in,
Withering everything with its plague,
Painting death upon leaves with acid-rain lacerations.
It's toxicity courses through my thinning frame.

Like a breath from Hel,
Winter sighs it's ice on my pale skin.
My clouded eyes are buried by snow.
Maggots whisper me goodnight.

I await the Spring sun.

It's Only Paper
R.M. Kent

It's a paper-back novel
In a paper bound world
Bout a paper bred boy
Or a paper doll girl

With paper proper ladies
In paper perfect pose
Makin paper wedding plans
An wearin paper clothes

Where paper pushin crooks
Are stealin priceless papers
An reading paper news
About their paper capers

An crouched in paper shelters
Are huddled paper people
Makin paper promises
Unto a paper steeple

A paper-made boss is
Givin out a paper raise
Like to papered puppies
Paper-trained for paper praise

We're takin paper trips
An ridin paper trains
Paper paid vacations
Via paper planes

We can't wear paper shoes
If the paper doesn't fit
Another paper junkie's
Getting torn to paper bits

An when the paper burn out
Sends you paper reeling
Only paper tears can
Come from paper feelings

Reflections
Derek L. Dugan

The fog grows thicker,
   Preventing me of sight.
Pain through my head
   That strains with all its might.

Cutting through the fields,
   The Reaper's wind still blows.
Stench fills the air
   As only dead should know.

Tread along the land
   As my body gives way.
Crash to the ground,
   May be my final day.

Blood covers my mail,
   Of others and my own.
Once full of rage,
   My body lies here prone.

Carnage surrounds me,
   Lifeless about the ground.
Screams in battle
   But now there's not a sound.

      I should continue moving,
      But find my mind astray,
      Reflecting on my life
      Here at my dying day.

Transcendence
Vincent D. Pisano

I am a man
Half of a whole
An opposing force
Destructive, awkward, brutal

She is a woman
Half of a whole
An opposing force
Delicate, graceful, beautiful

      As a key enters a lock we become
      As the moon eclipses sun
      Uniting in entwining limbs
      Till we two souls are one and none

      Through her womb I know creation
      By my shoulders she knows war
      Our pulses mingle, indistinguishable
      Desire showed us something more

      Ecstacy digs its nails
      Empyrean takes hold
      I pump my warm white soul
      Her body swallows

      For a moment I transcend thought
      And I know God

.
.
.
.
.
.
.
.

    Slowly, I become aware of my heaving chest
    The beads of sweat upon her breast

And I am a man again
Just half of a whole
An opposing force
Destructive, awkward, brutal

Avise la Fin?
Gabor J. Szabo

My walls bear a multitude of days etched with care.
Within the confines of my prison, I stack the reasons for being.
A high tide of doubt pulls and tugs at me ceaselessly.
Among the dank, rotten and foul, I am bewitched by my own demons.
Scraping, clawing and tearing the very seams of who I am.
The last bit of sunlight left me a long time ago.

Hope: a discipline I self-preach, a patience I try to instill within.
Nothing seems to break this bleak, foreboding gloom upon my chest.
My only light fed upon its own fuel long ago,
And lately I have encouraged darkness to saturate me, free me.

Where is the meaning for this existence?
Why am I wondering?
Why is God silent when I ask?
Why does He not answer His priest?
It's not supposed to happen this way…

My thoughts are losing their humanity, disoriented and torn by neglect.
Nowhere else to go,
Only wait here and face the torment of this rotting hell.
Troubled, I still dream of the sky,

Of the clouds floating above, and the people who look and wonder.

Etch another day on my coffin.

Cracked Rearview
Derek L. Dugan

I'm moving on
   And holding fast

Fuck you all
   I'm free at last

Now live my life
   For who I am

I'll reach for stars
   And all I can

You tried to take
   It all away

Kept pushing on
   Through every day

Can't take my life

            Can't take my pride

Can't take my will

            Can't take my drive.

Dryad's Dirge
Vincent D. Pisano

Salvation comes on cooling breeze,
    Heaven is evermore autumn,
I walk among the swirling leaves
    And descend with those that have fallen.

I lay amidst their flesh decay,
    Beside roots of gods in slumber,
Whose fingers shimmer with red-gold flames
    While ashy-paper drifts under.

I breathe deep the musky dirt,
    A scent old as Earthly time,
The home of kings, the home of worms,
    A home that will soon be mine.

Reminding us what October brings,
    Dryad's dirge is creaking wood,
I listen to the rustling sing
    The songs that no man ever could.

The Passion
R.M. Kent

Somewhere in time
Thought-lost in rhyme,
The poet wipes his brow.

Meanwhile afar,
Plays a guitar:
One minstrel holds a crowd.

Not to forget,
Her beads of sweat,
A dancer takes a bow.

Still another,
In-tense brother,
Is painting bold and proud.

They do not hide,
What lies inside,
Creating, in the now.

And so they live,
The gift they give,
The passion shows them how.

Acknowledgements

Poets Anonymous would first and foremost like to extend their heartfelt thanks to Kristen M. Pisano, for her constant support and input, and to Kaysa Cruse, for her time with us. We would also like to thank 202 Market Place in New Preston, CT, for allowing us the use of their premises afterhours to house our Open Mic Night.

We would also like to acknowledge and thank our fellow poets for their inspiration, and for adding something unique and positive to this world. Keep writing – brothers and sisters, saints and sinners, losers and winners, and sly-dawg mystic grinners. We hear you. We feel you. We are you.

And thanks to our readers for taking a chance on this book. We offer you the truth as we experience it. Take it or leave it. But believe it.

About the Authors

DEREK L. DUGAN is a co-partner and graphic web designer for Gibby Games, LLC, a gaming company in Danbury, CT. He enjoys writing songs, collecting comic books, and rebuilding classic muscle cars. He lives in New Milford, CT.

R.M. KENT is co-founder of Gibby Games, LLC, a gaming company in Danbury, CT. He has spent a majority of his life exploring the U.S., including hiking the Appalachian Trail. He currently resides in Florida where he has formed a new writing group.

VINCENT D. PISANO earned a B.A. in History at Western Connecticut State University and is an inductee of *Phi Alpha Theta* (History Honors Society, Inc.). His previous publication, *Looking Deeper*, was published by Yggdrasil Press, of which he is founder and chief editor. He spends his time traveling and studying history, philosophy and literature. He is currently an educator living with his wife, Kristen, in New Milford, CT.

GABOR J. SZABO, born in Hungary, served as a Sergeant in the Iraq War in the U.S. Army from 2003-2004. He became a U.S. citizen in 2005. He is currently studying history at Western Connecticut State University, and is an inductee of *Phi Alpha Theta* (History Honors Society, Inc.). His previous publication, *Army of One (Year +)*, was published by Yggdrasil Press. He spends his free time traveling and practicing photography. He is a co-partner of Gibby Games, LLC of Danbury, and lives in New Milford, CT.

Index of Poetry by Author

Derek L. Dugan

Ashes	25
Cracked Rearview	77
Illusions	65
In Case You Didn't Know	56
My Delilah	32
Reflections	72
The Minstrel and the Lyre	17
This Is What I Think of Your Exercise	54
Twilight	50
Yourself to Save	37

R.M. Kent

Block	15
It's Only Paper	70
Let Go	55
No Mor	45
No Partise Anum	62
Passion	79
Riky Tiky Tik	23
Taken	29
The Ballad of Mr. Hyde	39
Veni, Vedi, Arriverderci	18

Vincent D. Pisano

A Fresh-Red Kill	21
Crescent City Son	44
Dryad's Dirge	78
Fading	67
Loathéd	34
Oubliette	16
Roxanne of My Own	28
Sapphic Eden	53
[The Color of] Louisiana Steam	57
Transcendence	73

Gabor J. Szabo

Ant Hill	42
Avise la Fin?	75
Flakes of Ash	30
Her Waves	27
Janus-Side	46
Listless Years	69
Mason Dixon, Sr.	64
Nepenthe	36
Rain	19
Sum?	51

Amanda Armstrong

Hip-Hop: To My Mother   58

Megan O'Donnell

Breach   48

To order *It's Only Paper*, please visit the Yggdrasil Press website at:

www.yggdrasilpress.com

Or on MySpace at:

www.myspace.com/yggdrasilpress

One may also order directly from Lulu.com at:

www.lulu.com

To find out more about our group, please visit us on the web at:

www.myspace.com/anonymouspress

Also Available from **Yggdrasil Press!**

Army of One (Year +):
An Army Reservist in Iraq and Kuwait

Gabor J. Szabo

Take away the heroics and patriotism that are the main topics of books on war and you are left with the raw emotional conflicts that every soldier experiences. The aim of this book is to pull the reader into the mindset of an American soldier in the Iraq conflict through photographs and poetry, and hopefully leave one with a better understanding of the bullet holes which war leaves on the human condition.

Looking Deeper

Vincent D. Pisano

A collection of essays about religion, history, ethics, and politics.

www.ingramcontent.com/pod-product-compliance
Lightning Source LLC
LaVergne TN
LVHW011215080426
835508LV00007B/800